Foundations of Trading: Essential Knowledge for Beginners

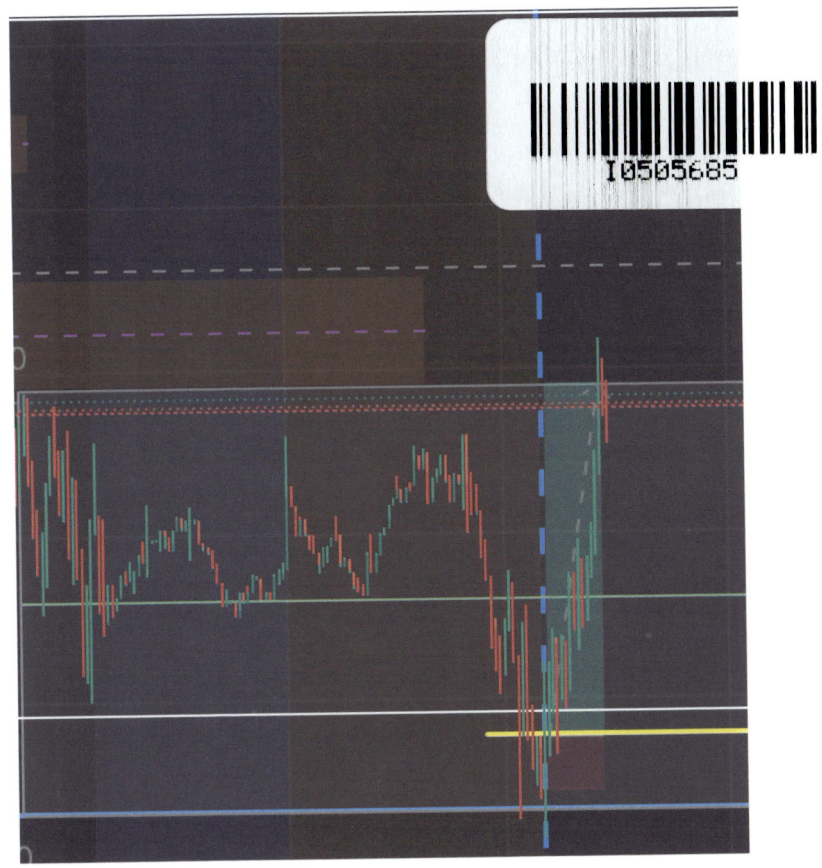

Authored by

Eiad Mohamed and Nader Beydoun

Financial Disclaimer

The information contained in this book is for educational and informational purposes only. The content is not intended to be and does not constitute financial, investment, or trading advice. The author and publisher are not financial advisors, and the information provided should not be considered a substitute for professional financial advice.

Trading and investing in financial markets involve risk, and it is possible to lose substantial amounts of money. The strategies and techniques discussed in this book are intended to provide general guidelines and examples, but they may not be suitable for every individual. It is important to conduct your own research, consider your financial situation, and consult with a qualified financial advisor before making any investment decisions.

The author and publisher make no representations or warranties about the accuracy, completeness, or suitability of the information provided. They shall not be held liable for any errors or omissions or for any damages arising from the use of or reliance on the information contained in this book.

Past performance is not indicative of future results. All investments carry risks, including the loss of principal. Readers are encouraged to seek professional advice and perform their own due diligence before making any financial decisions.

Table of Contents

Introduction..5

Chapter 1..9

Chapter 2: Trading Phycology...17

Chapter 3: Candle Sticks, Trends, And Structure.........24

Chapter 4 – Liquidity...34

Chapter 6 - How To Read And Comprehend News.....39

Chapter 7 - Trading Plan And Execution......................44

Chapter 8 - Back Testing And The Road To Trading

Live Capital...52

Chapter 9 - Extra Info, Don't Skip!................................55

Authors: Eiad Mohamed And Nader Beydoun............64

INTRODUCTION

Welcome to "Foundations of Trading: Essential Knowledge for Beginners

Purpose of this book

It is no surprise that trading is a very difficult endeavor, filled with much risk and uncertainties. Yet it also holds the potential for significant rewards and personal growth. The purpose of this book is to demystify the world of trading by walking you through each step of becoming a successful trader.

Who is this book for?

This book is designed for traders of all levels whether it be a very advanced trader trying to brush up on their skills or a beginner trying to learn for the first time. Whether you're interested in stock trading, Forex, Futures, or options, you will find practical advice in this book.

What Readers will learn

What Market is best for you: There will be detailed explanations on the major markets and which one is right for you.

Foundational Concepts: A thorough introduction to the basics of trading, including key terms and concepts essential for understanding the markets.

Developing a Strategy: Guidance on creating and implementing trading strategies, incorporating both technical and fundamental analysis.

Tools and Resources: An overview of the best trading platforms, tools, and resources available to traders, helping you make informed decisions.

Psychological Aspects: Insights into the psychological challenges of trading and how to cultivate the mindset of a successful trader.

Real-World Examples of concepts and trades: Examples to illustrate concepts and provide practical applications.

Disclaimer - it is important to remember that this is just one way of trading in these markets by no means is this the only way additionally, we only cover the basics.

Our Journeys

Eiad:

As a trader with years of experience navigating the highs and lows of the financial markets, I have amassed knowledge and insights that I am eager to share with you. My journey has been one of continuous learning, and it is my hope that this book will serve as a valuable resource on your own path to trading success.

Nader:

Although I started trading a little bit after Eiad did, over the past couple of years I have tested and failed at many different outlooks on trading which has led me to the concepts we will be teaching in this book. I'm hoping that this book can be a guiding light for any and all traders who come across it, allowing any reader to have a solid foundation in the financial markets.

Conclusion

Trading is a skill that can be learned and mastered with the right knowledge, discipline, and mindset. By the end of this book, you will have a solid foundation and a comprehensive toolkit to approach the markets. Let's embark on this journey together and unlock the potential that trading holds.

Chapter 1

What is Trading?

Trading is the act of buying and selling financial instruments with the aim of making a profit. These instruments can include stocks, bonds, currencies, commodities, and derivatives. Unlike long-term investing, trading often involves holding assets for a short period, from seconds to days or weeks.

Key Points:

Purpose: To generate profits by taking advantage of price movements.

Participants: Individual traders, institutional traders, market makers.

Types: Day trading (trading within the same day), swing trading (holding for several days or weeks), scalping (making numerous small trades to capture quick gains), and position trading (long-term trades based on broader market trends).

Examples:

Day Trading: A trader buys shares of a company in the morning and sells them in the afternoon or next couple of day.

Swing Trading: A trader buys stock after a significant price drop and holds it for several weeks until the price recovers.

Types of Markets

There are several types of financial markets where trading occurs, each with its own characteristics and opportunities.

1. Futures Markets

- Definition: Contracts to buy or sell an asset at a future date at a predetermined price.

- Common Assets: Commodities (oil, gold), indices (S&P 500), currencies.

- Characteristics: Highly leveraged, suitable for hedging and speculation.

- Example: A trader enters into a futures contract to buy 100 barrels of oil at $70 per barrel three months from now.

2. Forex Markets

- Definition: Trading of currencies from different countries against one another.

- Major Pairs: EUR/USD, USD/JPY, GBP/USD, AUD/USD.

- Characteristics: Largest and most liquid market, operates 24 hours a day across different time zones.

- Example: A trader buys euros (EUR) by selling US dollars (USD) expecting the euro to appreciate against the dollar.

3. Stock Markets

- Definition: Buying and selling shares of publicly traded companies.

- Major Exchanges: NYSE (New York Stock Exchange), NASDAQ, LSE (London Stock Exchange).

- Characteristics: Provides ownership in companies, influenced by company performance, economic indicators, and market sentiment.

- Example: An investor buys 100 shares of Apple (AAPL) stock, betting on the company's growth and profitability.

4. Cryptocurrency Markets

- Definition: Digital or virtual currencies traded on decentralized platforms.

- Popular Cryptos: Bitcoin (BTC), Ethereum (ETH), Ripple (XRP), Litecoin (LTC).

- Characteristics: High volatility, operates 24/7, decentralized with no central authority.

- Example: A trader buys Bitcoin expecting its price to rise due to increasing adoption and demand.

5. Options Markets

- Definition: Contracts giving the right, but not the obligation, to buy or sell an asset at a specific price before a certain date.

- Types: Call options (right to buy), put options (right to sell).

- Characteristics: Used for hedging, speculation, and leveraging positions.

- Example: A trader buys a call option for stock XYZ at a strike price of $50, expecting the stock price to exceed $50 before the option expires.

Differences Between Markets

Each market operates differently, with unique risks, rewards, and requirements:

- **Liquidity**: Forex markets are the most liquid, followed by futures, stocks, and cryptocurrencies. High liquidity means trades can be executed quickly with minimal price impact.

- **Trading Hours:** Stock markets have set trading hours (e.g., NYSE is open from 9:30 AM to 4:00 PM EST), while forex, futures, and crypto markets operate 24/7.

- **Leverage:** Futures and forex markets often offer higher leverage compared to stocks and cryptocurrencies, allowing traders to control larger positions with a smaller amount of capital.

- **Volatility:** Cryptocurrency markets are known for their high volatility, which can mean greater risk and reward. Stocks and forex can also be volatile, especially during economic announcements or geopolitical events.

Additional Considerations:

- **Regulation:** Stock and futures markets are highly regulated, ensuring transparency and investor protection.

Forex and cryptocurrency markets have varying levels of regulation, depending on the country.

- **Accessibility**: Forex and crypto markets are generally more accessible to individual traders due to lower capital requirements and 24/7 availability.

Understanding Options and the Greeks

Options trading involves understanding various metrics, often referred to as the "Greeks," which measure different risks associated with options:

1. **Delta (Δ):** Measures the sensitivity of the option's price to changes in the price of the underlying asset.

○ Example: A delta of 0.5 means the option price will move $0.50 for every $1 move in the underlying asset.

2. **Gamma (Γ):** Measures the rate of change of Delta with respect to changes in the underlying asset's price.

○ Example: High gamma indicates that delta will change rapidly as the underlying asset's price changes, affecting the option's price volatility.

3. **Theta (Θ):** Measures the sensitivity of the option's price to the passage of time (time decay).

o Example: A theta of -0.05 means the option's price will decrease by $0.05 each day, all else being equal.

4. **Vega (v):** Measures the sensitivity of the option's price to changes in the volatility of the underlying asset.

o Example: A vega of 0.10 means the option's price will increase by $0.10 for every 1% increase in implied volatility.

5. **Rho (ρ):** Measures the sensitivity of the option's price to changes in interest rates.

o Example: A rho of 0.02 means the option's price will increase by $0.02 for every 1% increase in interest rates.

If the Greeks are still unclear to you, we recommend watching a video on YouTube and researching further about it, in order to further your understanding. In addition to this, options are much more then this explanation, so if this is something you think you would like to do, you will need to research much further about it to grasp the concepts , this is just a brief overview of its components.

Market Theory

The main reason we trade and teach these concepts and strategies stems from our market theory. Our market theory is mainly based on information provided by Michael J. Huddleston AKA, The Inner Circle Trader. Although it isn't the exact same, we believe that the financial markets are run on a collection of algorithms whose sole purpose is the fulfillment of large institutional orders. This understanding is backed by 2 main reasons. Repeatability and time. To be profitable in trading with a mechanical strategy you need a repeatable process and if something in price repeats then there must be some sort of system at scale behind it. If price repeats a certain action at a certain time consistently then there must be a system. A simple example for the time aspect is to look at The 9:50 to 10:10 window on an asset like NQ1!, NASDAQ 100 futures ticker, and look for a reversal during this time window. Additionally if you are further interested in hard evidence besides logic then take the time to research the CLS and DTCC and their role in fulfilling orders at the institutional level, and at what time they fulfill them. We aren't going to go any deeper than that as at the end of the day all that matters is capital preservation and making money.

Chapter 2: Trading Phycology

The Importance of Trading Psychology

Before diving into the technical aspects of trading, it's crucial to understand the importance of trading psychology. This chapter will guide you through the psychological challenges you may face and how to manage them effectively.

Key Points:

Mental Preparedness: Trading can be emotionally taxing. Be prepared to face losing money, experiencing failure, and dealing with doubt from others who may not understand the trading world.

Expectations: Understand that success in trading doesn't come overnight. It requires time, patience, and resilience.

Emotional Resilience: The ability to recover from setbacks and remain focused on long-term goals is essential.

Example:

Losing Money: Every trader experiences losses. It's essential to accept this as part of the journey and not let it deter you.

Emotional Doubt: Friends and family might question your trading pursuits, but staying committed and focused on your goals is crucial.

Trading Psychology: 90% of the Game

Trading is often said to be 90% psychological and only 10% technical. Mastering your mindset is crucial to becoming a successful trader.

Key Aspects:

1. Risk Management:

- Always have a clear risk management strategy to protect your capital.

- Example: Setting stop-loss orders to limit potential losses and only risking a set percent of your account.

- Risk Tolerance: Understand your risk tolerance and never risk more than you can afford to lose.

2. Learning How to Lose:

- Accepting losses as part of trading and learning from them helps you stay emotionally balanced.

- Example: Avoid emotional reactions after a loss and analyze what went wrong to improve.

- o Emotional Detachment: Treat each trade as part of a larger strategy and avoid getting too emotionally attached to individual trades.

3. **Not Being Greedy:**

- o Greed can lead to poor decision-making and excessive risk-taking.
- o Example: Stick to your trading plan and avoid over-leveraging.
- o Moderation: Know when to take profits and not push for unrealistic gains.

4. **Knowing When to Win:**

- o Recognize and capitalize on profitable opportunities without becoming overconfident.
- o Example: Secure profits at predefined levels rather than aiming for unrealistic gains.
- o Confidence vs. Overconfidence: Maintain confidence in your strategy but remain humble and cautious.

5. **Knowing When to Trade:**

- o Only take trades when the conditions are favorable and align with your strategy.

- Example: Avoid trading during volatile market news unless you have a specific plan.

- Market Conditions: Understand different market conditions and adjust your strategy accordingly.

6. **Combating Revenge Trading:**

- Revenge trading occurs when you try to recover losses by making impulsive trades, often leading to more losses.

- Example: Take a break after a loss to clear your mind before making another trade.

- Self-Control: Develop the discipline to walk away and come back with a clear head.

Discipline

Discipline is the cornerstone of successful trading. It involves sticking to your trading plan, following your rules, and maintaining consistency in your actions.

Key Points:

Consistency: Develop and adhere to a consistent trading routine.

Rules: Establish and strictly follow your trading rules.

Self-Control: Maintain control over your emotions and decisions.

Routine: Set a daily routine that includes market analysis, reviewing your plan, and reflecting on your trades.

Example:

Trading Plan: Create a detailed trading plan and review it regularly to ensure you are on track.

Routine: Start your day with a review of the market news, analyze your positions, and adjust your plan as needed.

Patience and Long-Term Perspective:

Trading is not a get-rich-quick scheme. It will take months or even years to become consistently profitable. Patience is key to enduring the learning curve and developing your skills. You can get rich fast but not as quick as you think.

Key Points:

Learning Curve: Understand that becoming a successful trader takes time and effort.

Skill Development: Continuously improve your trading skills and knowledge.

Long-Term Goals: Focus on long-term goals rather than short-term profits.

Continual Learning: Stay updated with market trends, economic news, and new trading strategies.

Example:

Education: Invest time in learning through books, courses, and practice.

Mentorship: Seek out mentors or join trading communities to gain insights and feedback.

Avoiding the Quick Money Mindset:

One of the most common pitfalls in trading is the desire to make quick money. This mindset often leads to taking unnecessary risks and making impulsive decisions.

Key Points:

Realistic Expectations: Set realistic goals and understand that consistent profits come from disciplined trading, not from chasing quick gains.

Long-Term Success: Focus on building a sustainable trading strategy rather than seeking immediate rewards.

Risk Management: Implement robust risk management strategies to protect your capital.

Example:

Goal Setting: Establish achievable short-term and long-term goals to keep your trading journey on track.

Risk Management: Allocate only a small portion of your capital to high-risk trades and diversify your portfolio.

Strategy Hopping: Make sure that once you have explored your options to not "Strategy Hop" and stick with a strategy for at least a few months.

With all that said, understand that you're quite literally learning a skill that people spend their whole lives studying, it's not supposed to be easy. The best teacher for technicals and your Phycological space will ALWAYS be the charts and going through the arduous process of becoming a profitable trader. Always keep **your head up high and focus on the big picture, and with time and dedication, you'll get there.**

Chapter 3: Candle Sticks, trends, And Structure

What are candlesticks?

Candlesticks are a type of financial chart used to describe price movements of a security, derivative, or currency. Each candlestick represents a timeframe of price movement.

-For Example, each candlestick on this chart represents 30 Minutes of price movement on the S&P 500.

-Also, note how all these candlesticks form to create an Upwards Trend

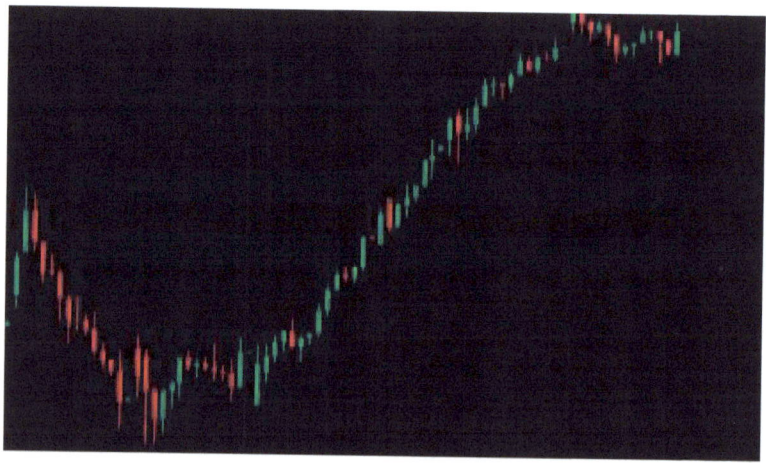

Components of a Candlestick:

Body: The thick part of the candlestick representing the range between the opening and closing prices.

Green or white Candlestick: Indicates that the closing price was higher than the opening price.

Red or black Candlestick: Indicates that the closing price was lower than the opening price.

Wicks (or Shadows): The lines extending above and below the body, representing the high and low prices of that trading period.

Upper Wick: The highest price reached during the trading period.

Lower Wick: The lowest price reached during the trading period.

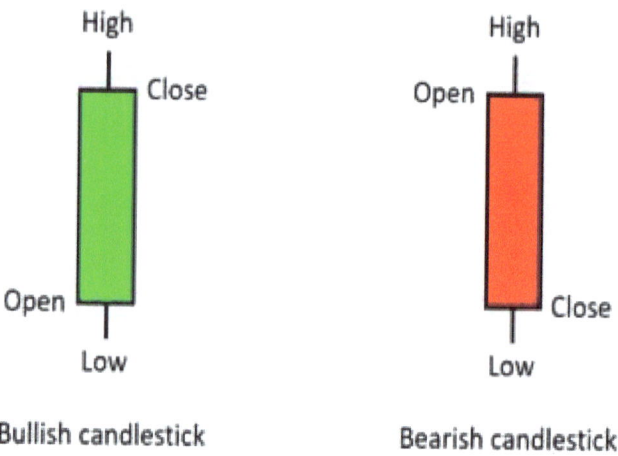

Bullish candlestick   Bearish candlestick

Anatomy of Candlesticks

Understanding the anatomy of candlesticks is crucial for interpreting price action and making informed trading decisions.

Open: The price at which the security first trades upon the opening of the trading period.

High: The highest price at which the security traded during the trading period.

Low: The lowest price at which the security traded during the trading period.

Close: The last price at which the security trades during the trading period.

Identifying Trends with Candlesticks

Candlesticks are powerful tools for identifying trends and patterns in the market. They provide visual cues that can help traders predict future price movements.

When understanding trends we can first visualize a line graph to structure our understanding.

Using Line Graphs to Show Trends:

Line Graph: A simple graph connecting closing prices over a specified period, providing a basic view of the overall trend.

Trend Identification: An upward trend is indicated by higher highs and higher lows, while a downward trend is indicated by lower highs and lower lows.

-The picture below of the S&P 500 Line Graph shows an upwards trend characterized by higher highs.

-Inversely if it was a downward trend it would be characterized by lower lows.

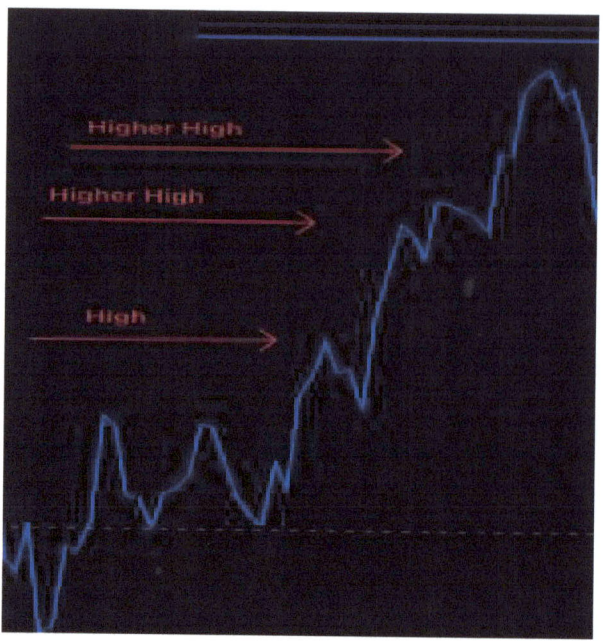

Transitioning to Candlesticks:

Candlestick charts offer more detailed information by showing the open, high, low, and close prices.

Bullish Trend: A series of green candlesticks with higher highs and higher lows.

Bearish Trend: A series of red candlesticks with lower highs and lower lows.

In the case of a candlestick chart a high is characterized by the highest point of an Upwards candle and a downwards candle And a low is characterized by the lowest point of a downwards candle and a upwards candle.

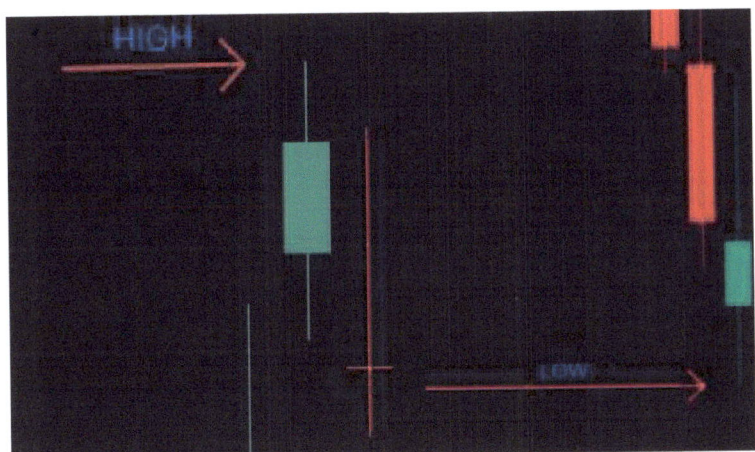

- **Therefore an upwards trend would be shown like this:**

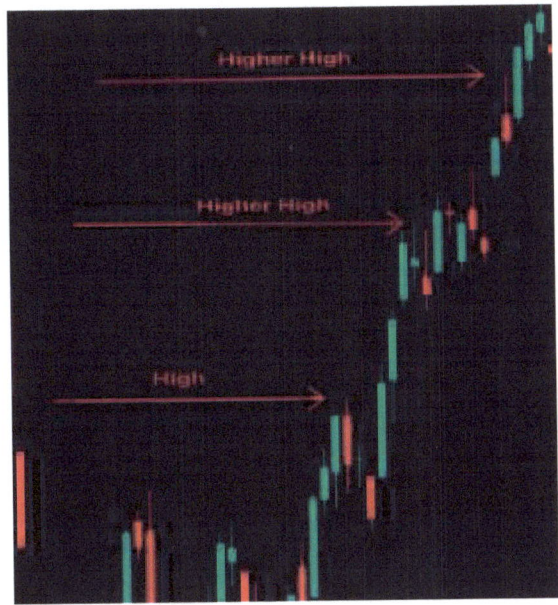

- **And an downward trend would be shown like this:**

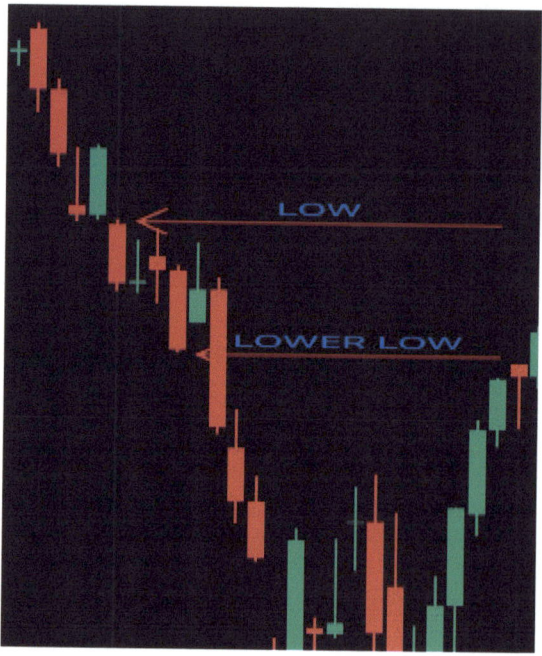

So in conclusion candlesticks are a tool to help analyze the market. The patterns and trends tell us when to buy and sell.

Break of structure (BOS) and how it's formed

Break of Structure: Occurs when the price closes above a swing high or low indicating a potential reversal or continuation of the trend.

Importance:

Trend Reversal: A BOS can signal the end of an existing trend and the beginning of a new trend.

Entry and Exit Points: Identifying BOS can help traders make informed decisions about when to enter or exit trades.

Example:

Uptrend BOS: The price closes above a high, confirming the continuation of the uptrend.

Downtrend BOS: The price closes below a low, confirming the continuation of the downtrend.

In This example, The Most recent High was closed above indicating a break in structure to the upside

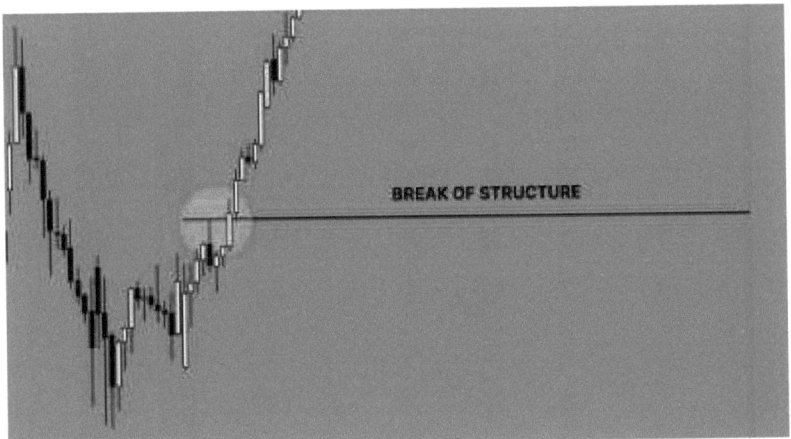

Another example:

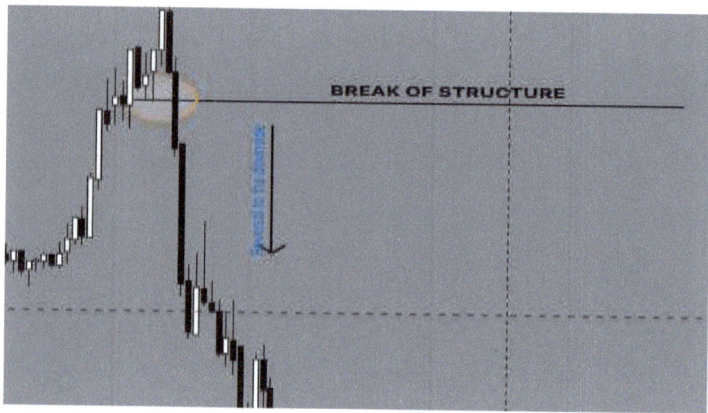

As we can see here price closes below the most recent low and reverses to the downside.

- Structure is created with the trend so if we are on an uptrend waiting for a possible reversal to the downside we would look for the most recent candle to close below our most recent low, therefore breaking the structure.

- And the same for reversal to the upside we would look for the most recent candlestick to close above the most recent high, therefore breaking the structure of the downward trend.

- Remember when using BOS that it is only a confluence and will not always be its own be a good predictor for market moves on its own.

Equilibrium

Equilibrium in trading is the middle of our current leg in price. In most cases price will retrace to at least equilibrium before continuing further. When trending upwards price will usually retrace half of the way up of the current leg in price. When trending downwards price will usually retrace half of the way down of the current leg in price. When your usingzEquilibrium to execute a trade for a short position you don't want to enter until your above equilibrium, and for longs you don't want to enter until you are below Equilibrium.

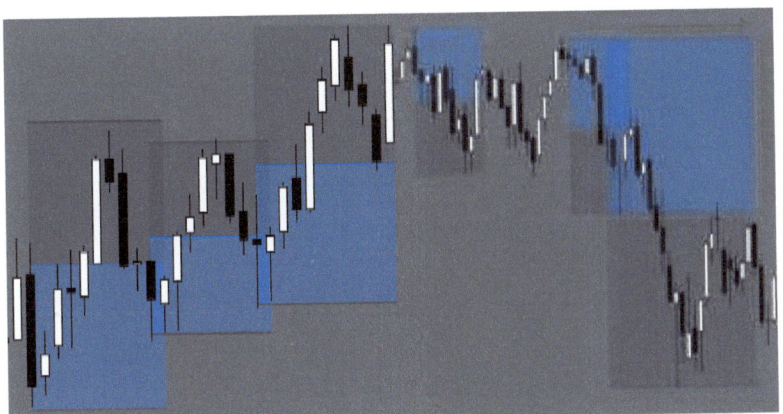

As seen in the first picture price retraces up at least half way before continuing downwards and in the second picture price retraces at least half way before continuing the uptrend.

Chapter 4 – liquidity

What is liquidity?

Liquidity is what price seeks out. As commented on previously in the Market Theory section, we believe price to be guided by algorithms whose main job is to fulfill large institutional orders. This can be seen in price when observing price for points of liquidity. Liquidity comes in many forms but we will mainly cover three. Highs and lows, fair value gaps, and order blocks. All of these will be covered

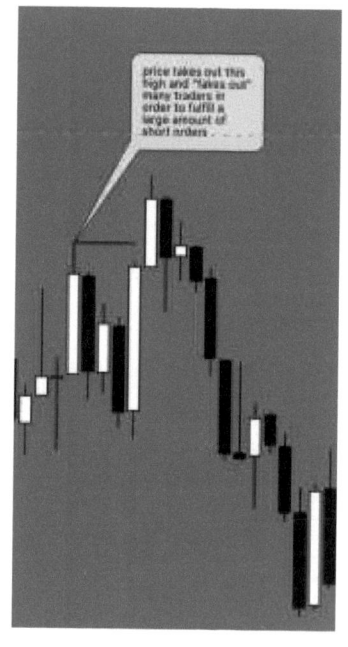

briefly here and more in depth in their own sections.

Highs and lows

Price will seek out stop losses that stack up at major highs and lows. Price will seek these out in order to fulfill institutional orders. This can be commonly seen or known as a fake out.

Fair value gaps

A fair value gap is a 3 candle sequence where the first and third candle wicks don't overlap. These can be used on the higher timeframe as points of interest for continuations and on the lower timeframe as an entry model. The candles don't need to be all going in the same direction and the second

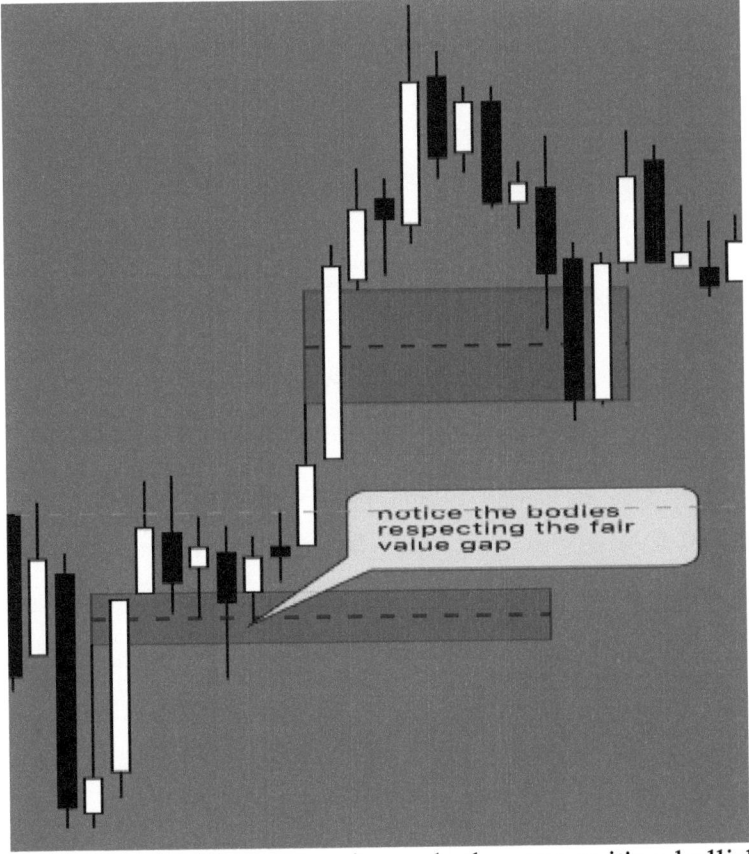

candle is the one that determines whether or not it's a bullish, support, bearish, resistance, fair value gap.

- In this image, you can see how the fair value gaps are used as support or resistance for continuations.

Order blocks

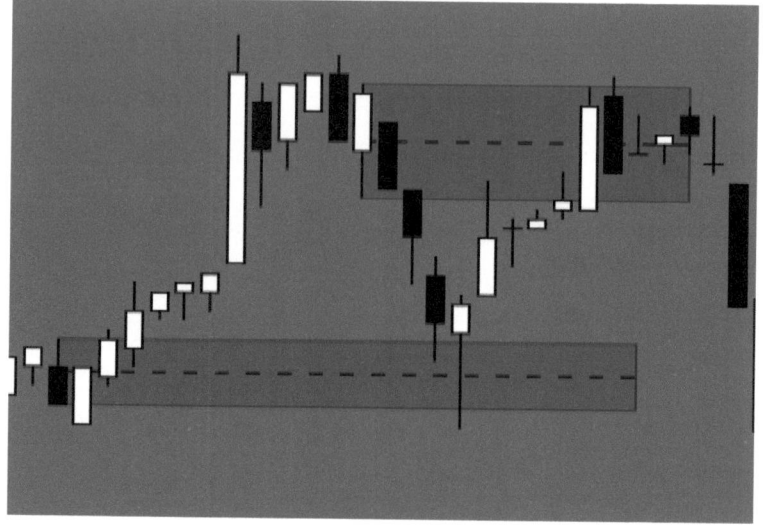

The opposing candle before a large move is an orderblock. For them to be high probability they need to have at least one of these two things. Taken liquidity or broken structure. They also must have fair value gaps after them. A Lot of the time price will fill in a fair value gap and respect it with its bodies and wick into the orderblock or rebalance a fair value gap and leave liquidity residing above the orderblock then come revisit it later for a continuation higher. price must also have a candle closure below the orderblock before it can be valid.

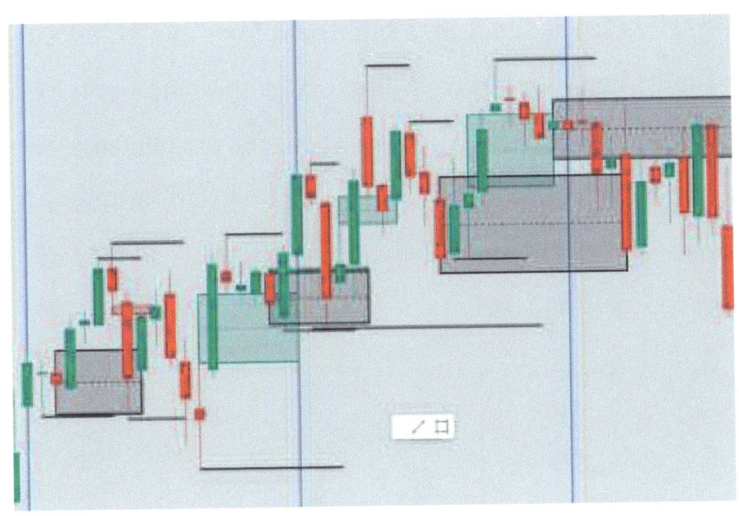

Highs and lows

High probability:

Monthly, Weekly, Daily, session, 4 hour, hourly

When looking for liquidity that price is targeting probable highs and lows are ones typically formed in a higher timeframe candle or range of time. These are important as they will usually represent major swing points in price and have large accumulation of stops by them.

Additionally, lower timeframe highs and lows can be used as a short-term liquidity target to frame a continuation entry off of or to look for deviations in price between correlated assets as well as identifying a low timeframe break of structure to use as an entry criterion when looking for a reaction of a time-based liquidity level.

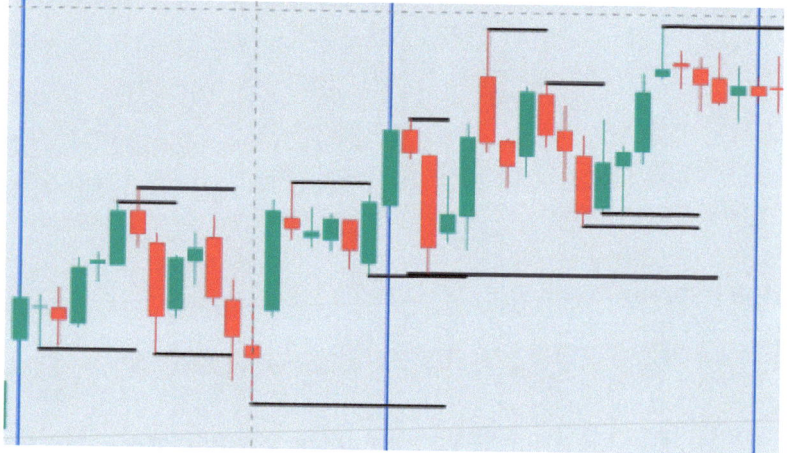

In this picture, the weekly and monthly highs and lows are all marked and you can see how price draws to high timeframe liquidity.

Chapter 6 - How to read and comprehend News

Although it is generally not recommended for traders to trade during news events due to increased volatility and unpredictability, if you choose to trade on news days, leveraging news can provide valuable insights into potential market movements.

We usually prioritize news events such as PPI (Producer Price Index), CPI (Consumer Price Index), unemployment rates, and FOMC (Federal Open Market Committee) announcements due to their significant impact on market movements. To effectively monitor these and other crucial news events, I recommend using Forex Factory. I will guide you through how to use this platform for optimal news tracking.

When you first open the website it will look like this but we need to customize it to our liking.

To access the filter options on the top right of the chart, follow these steps:

1. Go to Filter:

- Click on the filter icon located at the top right corner of the chart.

2. Customize Settings:

- You will see various customization options. For this example, I selected USD because I trade futures, and the USD is relevant to my trading strategy. Adjust the settings according to the market you are trading.

3. Filter for NYSE (New York Stock exchange) Trading:

- If you are trading on the NYSE, ensure that only USD is selected.
- Uncheck the yellow and grey boxes, as only the red and orange boxes highlight the most significant events.

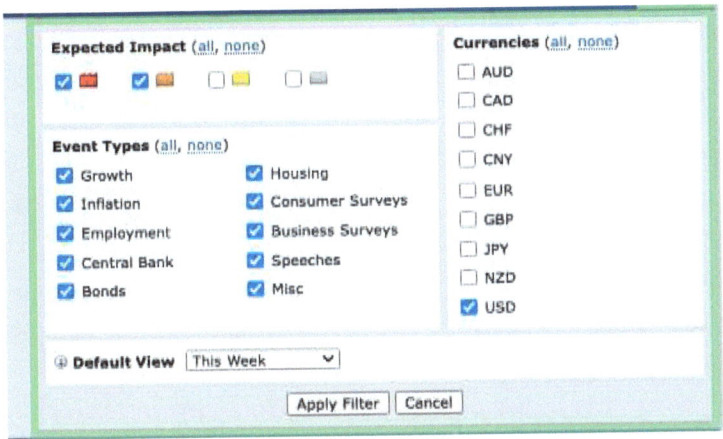

Now that our filters have been applied, let's take a look at a practical example. On Thursday, the Consumer Price Index (CPI) news was released, showing a lower-than-forecasted value. In simple terms, this means the CPI was lower than expected, which is favorable for the US market. Typically, a CPI reading lower than the forecast is positive for the US dollar (EG. the S&P 500 and NASDAQ will most likely rise), while a higher-than-forecast CPI is negative (EG. the S&P 500 and NASDAQ will most likely drop). This principle applies to other currencies as well.

For example, in the case of GBP/USD:

GBP/USD:

If the news is good for the GBP , the price of GBP/USD tends to rise.

If the news is bad for the GBP, the price of GBP/USD tends to fall.

Conversely, if the news is good for the USD , the price of GBP/USD tends to fall.

If the news is bad for the USD , the price of GBP/USD tends to rise.

Understanding these relationships helps traders anticipate market movements and make more informed trading decisions based on economic news.

Similarly, all economic forecasts impact the market based on the difference between the actual results and the forecasts. Essentially, any economic indicator that comes in lower than the forecast is typically good for the US market, while anything higher than the forecast is generally bad. Key indicators to watch include the CPI, PPI, FOMC decisions, and unemployment claims.

It's important to remember that trading based on news can be unpredictable. Even if an indicator appears positive or negative for the US market, market reactions can vary. Always approach news trading with caution due to its inherent volatility.

Disclaimer: Trading based on news can be highly unpredictable, and even seemingly good or bad news can lead to unexpected market reactions. Always ensure you have a robust risk management strategy in place when trading around news events.

Chapter 7 - Trading plan and execution

———◆———

Tying Everything Together: Forming a Daily Bias

To integrate all the concepts and strategies, let's follow a clear step-by-step process for forming a daily bias and identifying trade opportunities:

1. Form a Daily Bias:

Step 1: Start with the 4-hour chart on your charting platform (e.g., TradingView).

Step 2: Determine the trend direction on the 4-hour chart.

Example: If the 4-hour chart has broken structure to the upside, indicating higher highs and higher lows, the bias is bullish. Conversely, if it has broken structure to the downside, indicating lower highs and lower lows, the bias is bearish.

2. Align the 1-Hour Chart:

Step 3: Check the 1-hour chart to see if it aligns with the 4-hour trend.

Alignment: If the 1-hour chart also shows a bullish trend (higher highs and higher lows) or a bearish trend (lower highs and lower lows), it confirms the daily bias.

3. Scaling Down for Trade Entries:

Step 4: If the 1-hour chart aligns with the 4-hour chart:

Action: Scale down to the 5-minute chart to identify precise entry points.

Step 5: If the 1-hour chart does not align with the 4-hour chart:

Action: Scale down to the 15-minute chart to find more granular entry signals and confirm potential trade setups.

In this example, we can see that we are bullish on the 4hr making our daily bias bullish. Now we will scale down to the 1hr and check to see if it confirms our daily bias.

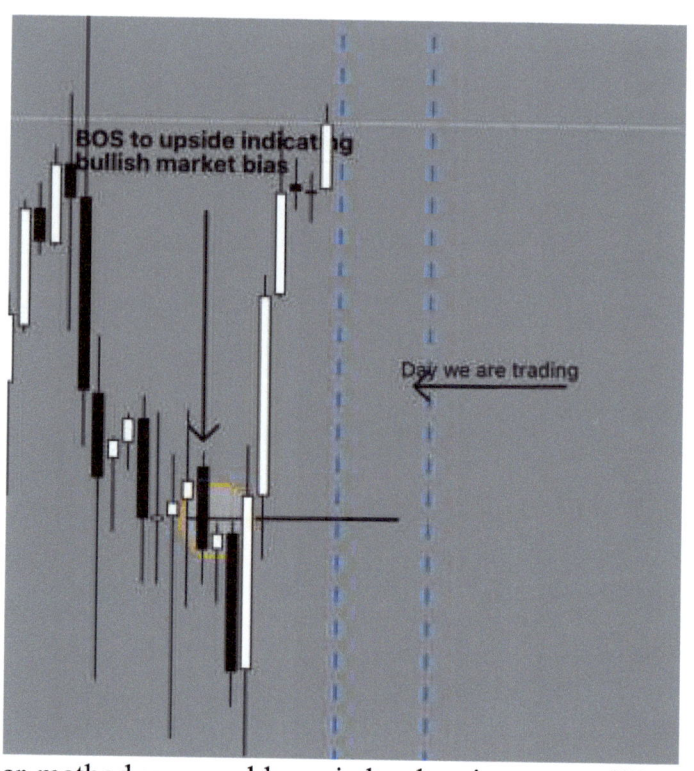

Another method you could use is by drawing an equilibrium level. On TradingView, you can use a "Gann Box" and focus on the 0.5 mark to identify equilibrium. This level indicates that the price has reached a discounted price and is continuing upwards, which aligns with our Break of Structure (BOS) bias.

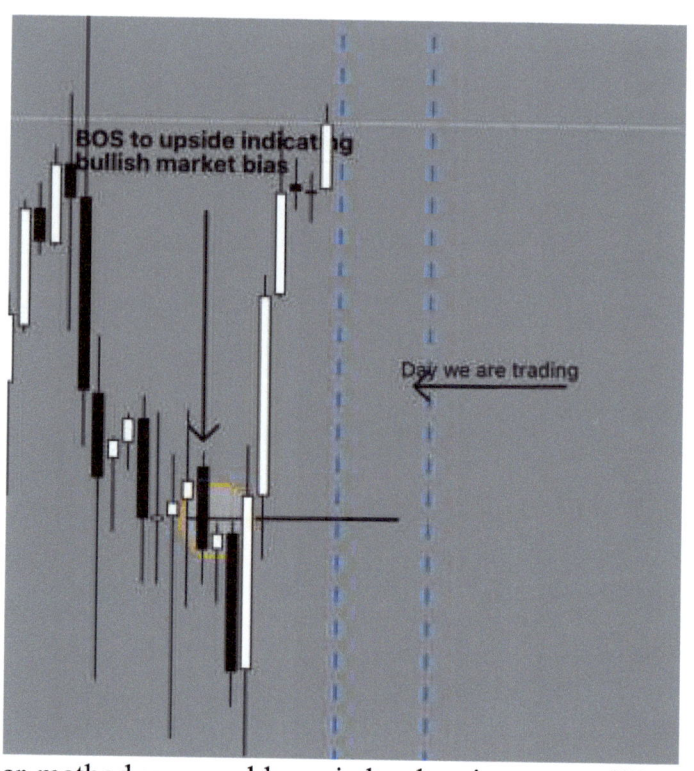

The next step, after determining your daily bias, is to scale into the 1-hour chart to see if it aligns with the 4-hour trend. If the 1-hour chart aligns with the 4-hour chart, we can then start identifying liquidity areas for execution. However, if the 1-hour chart shows a bearish trend, which contradicts our 4-hour bullish bias, we will scale down to the 15-minute chart and look for trade opportunities using the 1-hour bearish bias.

- Since we have confirmed that the 1-hour chart is also bullish, the next step is to mark out the most recent low. We will monitor this point for a price sweep and an upward movement, aligning with our bullish bias.

- If we are looking for the price to move up, we identify liquidity by marking the most recent low, which includes a down candle followed by an up candle. Conversely, if we want the price to move down, we mark the most recent high, which includes an up candle followed by a down candle.

- When in a trade, focus on marking the most recent liquidity points. This helps in identifying potential entry and exit points based on the expected market movements towards these liquidity zones.

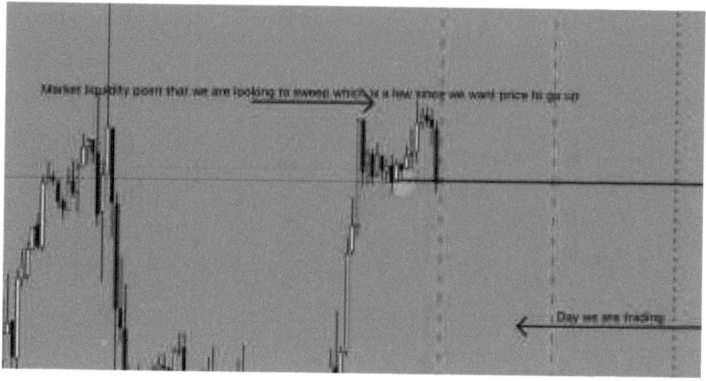

Now, since we have our setup we will go to the 5 minute chart and watch for our execution so we are going to wait for a BOS after a liquidity sweep.

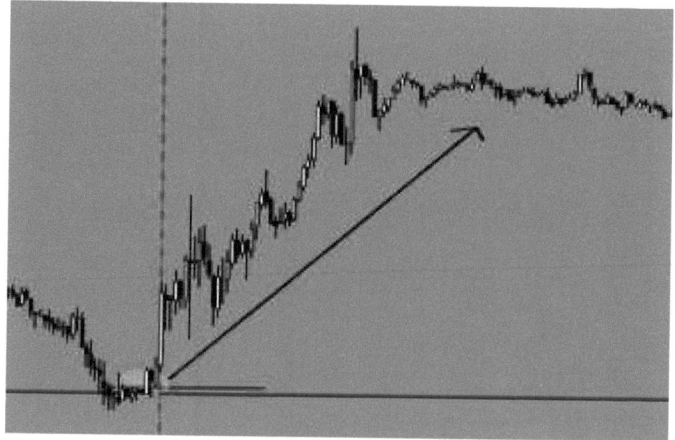

As we can see from this example, the market swept liquidity and then broke structure, providing a good entry point at market open. This illustrates how everything flows together and is organized effectively. Typically, you want to find a third confluence to be absolutely sure of your entry.

Additional Confluences:

Order Block: Identify the last opposing candle before a significant move. This area can act as a strong support or resistance.

Equilibrium: Use tools like the Gann Box to find the 0.5 mark, indicating equilibrium. This level often acts as a pivotal point where price might reverse or continue its trend.

Fair Value Gap (FVG): Look for gaps between candles where there is no overlap. These gaps often act as support or resistance zones.

Scaling Down for Perfect Entry:

Right before you execute the trade, you can scale down to the 1-minute chart. This allows you to see finer details and get a more precise entry point, ensuring optimal timing.

By combining the sweep of liquidity, break of structure, and an additional confluence like an order block, equilibrium, or FVG, you significantly increase the probability of a successful trade. Always look for that third confirmation to enhance your confidence in the trade setup.

Example:

You can also trade intraday using shorter timeframes, such as the 5-minute chart, based on retracements. For example, this particular trade was made using a fair value gap, with the take-profit target set at the most recent liquidity point. This approach allows you to capture quick gains while still adhering to your overall trading strategy.

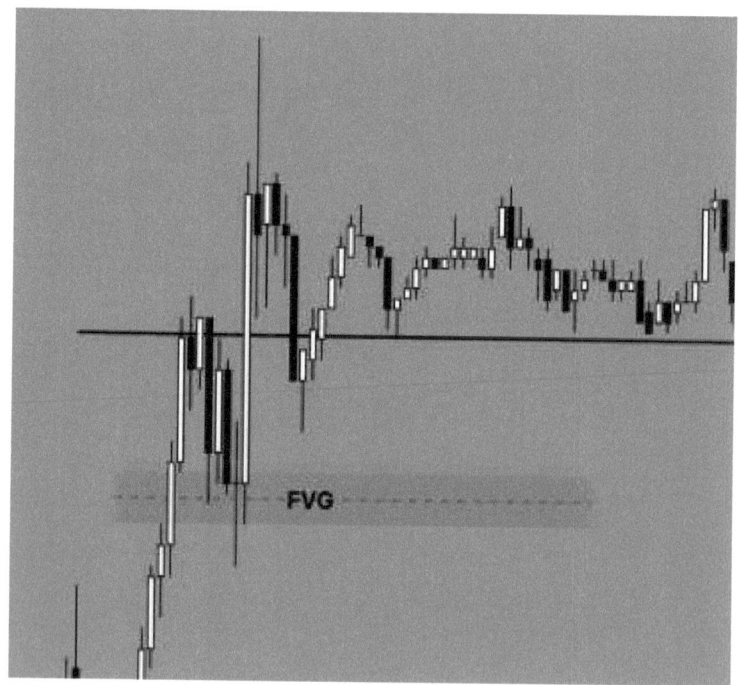

STRATEGY

- Start with daily bias
- Then watch 1 Hr for liquidity
- Then scale into 15 min if 1 Hr does not follow 4hr
- Then scale into 5 min if 1 Hr follows 4 Hr bias
- Wait for liquidity sweep
- Watch for BOS
- Then wait for preferably 3rd confluence then execute

Chapter 8 - Back testing and the road to trading live capital

———————◆———————

Back testing

You aren't going to become a profitable trader by just reading this book. You need to actively put the information you learn here into action and test everything for yourself. The best way to do this is through back testing on either Trading View or on a website like FX Replay.

Platforms: You can back test on Trading view with their basic paid plan or FX Replay which is more expensive but it collects and compiles your data with statistics for you.

When you're back testing you aren't just looking at previous price action and marking random stuff. You need to decide on what you want to test, mark it out, then wait to see what the price does when you let it go forward in time.

Additionally you should be tracking your data in a spread sheet to know if the strategy is profitable or not. Your data should be from at least 1 years worth of trades.

The whole point behind back testing is to simulate live price at a much quicker pace and at your convenience.

An example that you should go try-

Go back in time by a year and every day before the market opens mark the most obvious swing highs in our current range, mark out bearish and bullish FVGS, and Order blocks. Do all of this on the 1h and 4h Now look for price to reach one of your levels between market open, 9:30 am EST, and 11:30 am and provide a break of structure on the 5m timeframe and then retrace into a 5m fair value gap that should be created in that price leg that broke structure. Stop loss could be at the high or low of the leg the FVGs is in and you could do a 1:2 risk to reward or target opposing liquidity.

As seen in this example we approach price with a plan and strategy and wait for our entry opportunity to be provided. By doing this you can go into back testing with a real plan and take away valuable experience

Paper trading

Once you have back-tested different strategies and concepts you can move on to paper trading. Paper trading is when you trade live price action but on simulated funds. When you paper trade you should use an account size that would reflect what you would do on live and have the same risk or there'd be no point. The main difference between this and back testing is that you will have to watch price print live and wait for price to either stop you out or hit your take profit. It will take longer but if you can take a strategy that's profitable in back testing and then replicate the results on demo for at least 3 you will know that you're ready for a live personal account or prop firm account.

Chapter 9 : extra info, don't skip!

Time

When trading futures or forex you should almost always have a time window you trade in. When deciding this you should look at your asset you are trading and its correlated market session

The market sessions are the Asian session, London session, and NY session.

Asian session opens at 20:00 UTC -4 (est time), London opens at 03:00 UTC -4, New York opens at 09:30 utc-4. The times for asian and london will be different in the US when there aren't daylight savings. London will be at 19:00 UTC -5 and Asia will be at 02:00 UTC -5. These opens are based on major exchange opens and injections of volatility and volume.

If you're trading any asset correlated with the dollar you should be trading around New York Open. If you're trading anything GBP, EUR based, or any European based currency you should trade during or around London open. If you are trading anything JPY based or Australian based you should trade Asian session.

New York and London sessions usually contain the largest moves while Asian usually consolidates and ranges.

Content

All the content provided in this book is all the basics and fundamentals. Although this is all you need, if you want to learn more you should watch ICT and TJRtrades.

Remember

You need to be committed to your trading journey and be willing to put in the time. Trading isn't very complicated, it is just as hard a skill to learn and a long process. The most important part of all of this is being consistent. You have to stick with it.

Word bank

Bearish Trend: A market condition where prices are generally falling, characterized by lower highs and lower lows.

Bid Price: The highest price a buyer is willing to pay for a security.

BOS (Break of Structure): Occurs when the price breaks through a significant support or resistance level, signaling a potential trend reversal or continuation.

Bullish Trend: A market condition where prices are generally rising, characterized by higher highs and higher lows.

Call Option: A financial contract that gives the buyer the right, but not the obligation, to buy a security at a specified price within a specified time period.

Candlestick: A type of financial chart representing price movements within a specified time frame. Each candlestick shows the open, high, low, and close prices.

Close Price: The last price at which a security trades during the trading period.

Consumer Price Index (CPI): An economic indicator measuring the average change in prices paid by consumers for goods and services.

Day Trading: A trading strategy where traders buy and sell securities within the same trading day.

Delta (Δ): Measures the sensitivity of the option's price to changes in the price of the underlying asset.

Discipline: The ability to follow a trading plan and maintain consistency in trading actions and decisions.

Diversification: A risk management strategy that involves spreading investments across various assets to reduce exposure to any single asset or risk.

Doji: A candlestick with a small body, indicating indecision in the market.

Emotional Resilience: The ability to recover from setbacks and remain focused on long-term goals.

Equilibrium: The midpoint of the current price leg. Price often retraces to this level before continuing its trend.

Fair Value Gap: A three-candle sequence where the wicks of the first and third candles do not overlap. This gap indicates an imbalance in buying or selling pressure, often serving as a support or resistance level.

FOMC (Federal Open Market Committee): A branch of the Federal Reserve responsible for setting monetary policy, including interest rates.

Forex (Foreign Exchange) Market: A global marketplace for exchanging national currencies against one another.

Gamma (Γ): Measures the rate of change of Delta with respect to changes in the underlying asset's price.

Greed: An excessive desire for profit that can lead to poor decision-making and excessive risk-taking.

High Price: The highest price at which a security traded during the trading period.

Interest Rates: The cost of borrowing money, typically expressed as a percentage of the amount borrowed.

Leverage: The use of borrowed funds to increase the potential return on investment.

Liquidity: The ease with which an asset can be bought or sold in the market without affecting its price. High liquidity indicates a large number of buyers and sellers.

Liquidity Sweep: A price movement that triggers stop-loss orders at significant highs or lows, often resulting in a sharp price reversal.

Low Price: The lowest price at which a security traded during the trading period.

Market Makers: Entities that provide liquidity to the market by being ready to buy and sell securities at any time, profiting from the bid-ask spread.

Market Sentiment: The overall attitude of investors towards a particular security or financial market, influencing their trading decisions.

Mentorship: Seeking guidance and advice from experienced traders to gain insights and improve trading skills.

Moderation: Knowing when to take profits and not push for unrealistic gains.

Option Contract: A financial contract that gives the buyer the right, but not the obligation, to buy or sell a security at a specified price within a specified time period.

Order Block: The last candle in the opposite direction before a significant price move. It acts as a supply or demand zone where price is likely to react upon revisiting.

Paper Trading: Practice trading with a simulated account using real-time market data, allowing traders to develop and test strategies without risking real money.

Patience: The ability to wait for favorable market conditions and avoid impulsive trading decisions.

PPI (Producer Price Index): An economic indicator measuring the average change in selling prices received by domestic producers for their output.

Position Trading: A long-term trading strategy where positions are held for months or even years, based on broader market trends.

Put Option: A financial contract that gives the buyer the right, but not the obligation, to sell a security at a specified price within a specified time period.

Resistance Level: A price level where an uptrend can be expected to pause due to a concentration of supply.

Revenge Trading: Making impulsive trades in an attempt to recover losses, often leading to further losses.

Rho (ρ): Measures the sensitivity of the option's price to changes in interest rates.

Risk Management: Techniques and strategies used to minimize financial losses, such as setting stop-loss orders, diversifying portfolios, and managing position sizes.

Scalping: A trading strategy involving numerous small trades to capture quick gains, typically within minutes.

Self-Control: The ability to maintain control over emotions and decisions in trading.

Stop-Loss Order: An order placed to sell a security when it reaches a certain price, used to limit an investor's loss on a position.

Support Level: A price level where a downtrend can be expected to pause due to a concentration of demand.

Swing Trading: A trading strategy where positions are held for several days or weeks to capitalize on expected price movements.

Technical Analysis: The study of past market data, primarily price and volume, to forecast future price movements.

Theta (Θ): Measures the sensitivity of the option's price to the passage of time (time decay).

Trading Psychology: The study of the emotional and mental aspects of trading and how they affect decision-making and performance.

Trend Identification: The process of determining the overall direction of the market, typically categorized as uptrend, downtrend, or sideways trend.

Vega (v): Measures the sensitivity of the option's price to changes in the volatility of the underlying asset.

Volatility: A statistical measure of the dispersion of returns for a given security or market index, indicating the degree of variation in trading prices over time.

Authors: Eiad Mohamed and Nader Beydoun

Thank you to **Mohamed Lotfy** for Co-Editing and reviewing this book

Service used for charting: TradingView

Service used for news: Forexfactory